T0056375

iPhone®
PORTABLE GENIUS
SIXTH EDITION

Paul McFedries

WILEY

This book is dedicated to my beautiful wife, Karen,
who is wise, funny, and smart, even in texts.

About the Author

Paul McFedries is a full-time technical writer. Paul has been authoring computer books since 1991 and has nearly 100 books to his credit. Paul's books have sold more than four million copies worldwide. These books include the Wiley titles *Windows Portable Genius; iPad Portable Genius,* Fourth Edition; *Teach Yourself VISUALLY Windows 10,* Third Edition; and *G Suite for Dummies.* You can visit Paul on the web at www.mcfedries.com or on Twitter at www.twitter.com/paulmcf.

Acknowledgments

I had a great time writing this book because it's just pure fun to write about what's new and noteworthy in the iPhone, particularly the lesser-known features that can make your life easier and more efficient. More than that, however, I got to work with a great bunch of professionals at Wiley. There's a long list of people who contributed to the making of this book, and I extend a hearty thanks to all of them for their hard work and competence. A few of those people I had the pleasure of working with directly included Associate Publisher Jim Minatel, Project Editors Maureen and Scott Tullis, Copy Editor Kim Wimpsett, and Content Refinement Specialist Barath Kumar Rajasekaran. Many thanks to each of you for the skill, professionalism, sense of humor, and general niceness that made my job infinitely easier and made this a better book.

Contents

chapter 3

How Do I Connect My iPhone to a Network? 46

chapter 4

How Can I Get More Out of the Phone App? 64

chapter 5

How Can I Make the Most of iPhone Web Surfing?   80

chapter 6

How Do I Maximize iPhone Email?   104

Introduction

The iPhone is a success not because more than 2 billion of them have been sold (or, I should say, not *only* because over 2 billion of them have been sold; that's a *lot* of phones!), but because the iPhone has reached the status of a cultural icon. Even people who don't care much for gadgets in general and cell phones in particular know about the iPhone. For those of us who do care about gadgets, the iPhone elicits a kind of technological longing that can be satisfied in only one way: by buying one.

Part of the iconic status of the iPhone comes from its gorgeous design and remarkable interface, which makes all the standard tasks — surfing, emailing, texting, scheduling, and playing — easy and intuitive. But just as an attractive face or an easygoing manner can hide a personality of complexity and depth, so too does the iPhone hide many of its most useful and interesting features.

When you want to get beyond the basics of iPhone and solve some of its riddles, you might know some iPhone geniuses in person or online. Ideally, you'll get good advice on how to get your iPhone to do what you want it to do. Asking a genius is a great thing, but it isn't always a convenient thing because geniuses often have better things to do with their time.

What you really need is a "genius" of your own that's easier to access, more convenient, and doesn't require pleading emails or bribery. What you really need is a portable genius that enables you to be more productive and solve problems — wherever you and your iPhone happen to be.

Welcome, therefore, to *iPhone Portable Genius,* Sixth Edition. This book is kind of a genius all wrapped up in an easy-to-use, easy-to-access, and eminently portable format. In this book, you learn how to get more out of your iPhone by accessing all the powerful and timesaving features that aren't obvious at a casual glance. In this book, you learn about all the amazing new features found in the latest iPhones and the latest version of iOS. In this book, you learn how to prevent iPhone problems from occurring and (just in case your preventative measures are for naught) how to fix many common problems.

This book is for iPhone users who know the basics but want to take their iPhone education to a higher level. It's a book for people who want to be more productive, more efficient, more creative, and more self-sufficient (at least as far as the iPhone goes). It's a book for people who use their iPhone every day but would like to incorporate it into more of their day-to-day activities. It's a book I had a blast writing, so I think it's a book you'll enjoy reading.

How Do I Start Using My iPhone?

When you first look at your iPhone, you notice its sleek, curvaceous design, and then you notice what might be its most remarkable feature: It's nearly button-free! Unlike your garden-variety smartphone bristling with keys and switches and ports, your iPhone has very few physical buttons. This makes for a stylish, possibly even sexy, design, but it also leads to an obvious problem out of the box: How do you work the darn thing? This chapter solves that problem by giving you the grand tour of your iPhone. You learn about the few physical buttons on the phone, and then I show you the real heart of the iPhone, the remarkable touchscreen.

Working with the Side Button

If your iPhone is on but you're not using it, the phone automatically goes into standby mode after one minute. This is called Auto-Lock, and it's a handy feature because it saves battery power when your iPhone is just sitting there. However, you can also put your iPhone into standby mode at any time by using the Side button (also called the Sleep/Wake button). As pointed out in Figure 1.1, you find this button on the right side of your phone, assuming you're holding the phone as shown in Figure 1.1 (this is called *portrait* orientation). (On older iPhones, the Side button is on the top of your phone.)

1.1 On all recent iPhone models, the Side button appears on the right side.

As I describe in the following sections, the Side button has four main functions: sleeping and waking, powering on and off, handling incoming calls, and authorizing purchases.

Sleeping and waking the iPhone

If you're currently using your iPhone, you put the phone in standby mode by pressing the Side button once. You can still receive incoming calls and texts, but the screen powers down, which drops the power consumption considerably. Tap the Side button again to wake your iPhone (or just tap the screen). You're prompted with the Swipe Up to Open message shown in Figure 1.1, and you slide your finger up from the bottom of the screen to unlock the phone (or enter your passcode).

Genius

> Press the Side button to put your phone in standby whenever you're not using the screen. This not only conserves battery power but also prevents accidental screen taps. If you have a program such as the Music app running, it continues to run even while the phone is in standby.

Powering the iPhone on and off

You can also use the Side button to turn off your iPhone so that it uses no power. This is a good idea if your battery is getting low and you don't think you'll be able to charge it any time soon. You can still periodically check your messages or make an outgoing call when needed, but as long as you turn off the phone when you're done, you minimize the chance that your battery will drain completely. You might also want to turn off your iPhone if you won't be using it for a few days.

Follow these steps to turn off your iPhone:

1. **Press and hold both the Side button and either the Volume Up or Volume Down button (pointed out in Figure 1.1) for a couple of seconds.** The Slide to Power Off slider appears on the screen, as shown in Figure 1.2. For the record, note that this screen also comes with three other features of note:

   - **Medical ID.** Drag this slider all the way to the right to open the Medical ID page, which shows your name, your date of birth, and your medical conditions, allergies, medications, blood type, and more. To configure your Medical ID page, open Settings, tap Health, and then tap Medical ID.

   - **Emergency SOS.** Drag this slider all the way to the right to place a call to your local emergency service (such as 911) and, once the call ends, to optionally send an emergency text to each person listed in the Health app's Emergency Contacts list. To configure Emergency SOS, open Settings and tap Emergency SOS.

- **Cancel.** Tap this button if you change your mind and decide to leave your iPhone on.

2. **Use your finger to drag Slide to Power Off all the way to the right.** The iPhone shuts down after a few seconds.

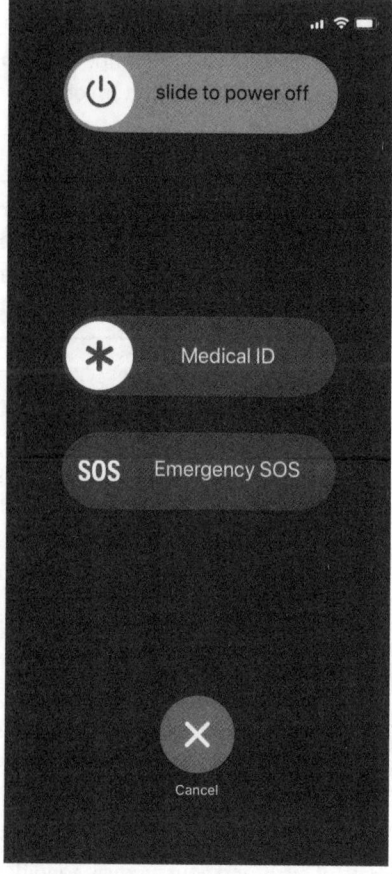

1.2 Press and hold the Side button and a Volume button to display this screen.

When you're ready to resume your iPhone chores, press and hold the Side button until you see the Apple icon. The iPhone powers up and then a few seconds later displays the unlock screen.

Silencing or declining a call

The Side button has another couple of tricks up its electronic sleeve, and these features give you quick ways to handle incoming calls:

- **Silence an incoming call.** Press the Side button once. This temporarily turns off the ringer, which is great in situations where you don't want to disturb the folks around you. You still have the standard four rings to answer, should you decide to. If you don't answer, your iPhone sends the call to your voicemail.

- **Decline an incoming call.** Press the Side button twice. This sends the call directly to voicemail, which is useful in situations where you don't want the ringing to disturb your neighbors and you don't want to answer the call. Note that, in this case, you don't have the option of answering the call.

Making a purchase

If your iPhone has Face ID, you also use the Side button to make purchases:

- **Use Apple Pay in a store.** Double-click the Side button to use your default Apple Pay card. For more about Face ID and setting up Apple Pay, see Chapter 2.

- **Confirm an app or in-app purchase.** Wait until you see the Double Click to Confirm prompt shown in Figure 1.3; then double-click the Side button to authorize the purchase.

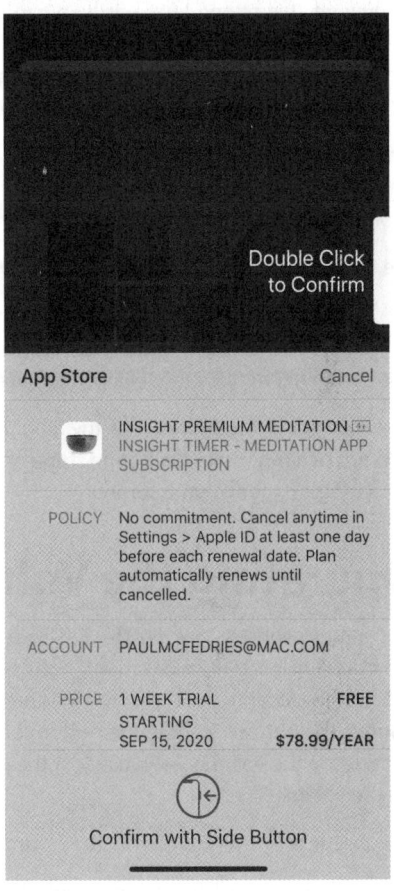

1.3 Double-click the Side button to authorize an app or in-app purchase.

Working with the Ring/Silent Switch

When a call comes in and you press the Side button once, your iPhone silences the ringer. That's great if you're in a meeting or a movie, but the only problem is that it may take you one or two rings before you can tap the Side button, and by that time the folks nearby are already glaring at you.

To prevent this phone faux pas, you can switch your iPhone into Silent Mode, which means it doesn't ring, and it doesn't play any alerts or sound effects. When the sound is turned off, only alarms that you've set using the Clock application will sound. The phone will still vibrate unless you turn this feature off as well.

You switch the iPhone between Ring Mode and Silent Mode using the Ring/Silent switch, which is located on the left side of the iPhone, near the top (assuming you're holding the phone in portrait orientation), as shown earlier in Figure 1.1.

Use the following techniques to switch between Silent Mode and Ring Mode:

- **Put the phone in Silent Mode.** Flick the Ring/Silent switch toward the back of the phone. You see an orange stripe on the switch, the iPhone vibrates briefly, and you see a brief notification telling you that Silent Mode is on.

- **Return to Ring Mode.** Flick the Ring/Silent switch toward the front of the phone. You no longer see the orange stripe on the switch, and the iPhone displays the current ringer volume setting.

Operating the Volume Controls

The volume controls are on the left side of the iPhone (again, when you're holding the phone in portrait orientation), right below the Ring/Silent switch (see Figure 1.1). The button closer to the top of the iPhone is Volume Up, and you press it to increase the volume; the button closer to the bottom of the iPhone is Volume Down, and you press it to decrease the volume. As you adjust the volume, a slider appears on-screen representing the volume level.

You use these buttons to control the volume throughout your iPhone:

- If you're on a call, the volume controls adjust your speaker volume.

- If you're using the Music app, the volume controls adjust the music volume.

- In all other situations, the volume controls adjust the output of sounds such as alerts and effects.

8

Inserting a SIM Card

Before you can use your iPhone to make and receive calls over the cellular network, you need to insert a SIM (subscriber identity module) card, which your cellular provider includes with your phone (or which you can purchase separately as a prepaid card).

With your SIM card at hand, follow these steps to insert it into your iPhone:

1. **Locate the SIM removal tool that came with your phone.** Figure 1.4 points out this tool. If you can't find the SIM removal tool, you can use any object with a similarly narrow end, such as a small paperclip or a safety pin.

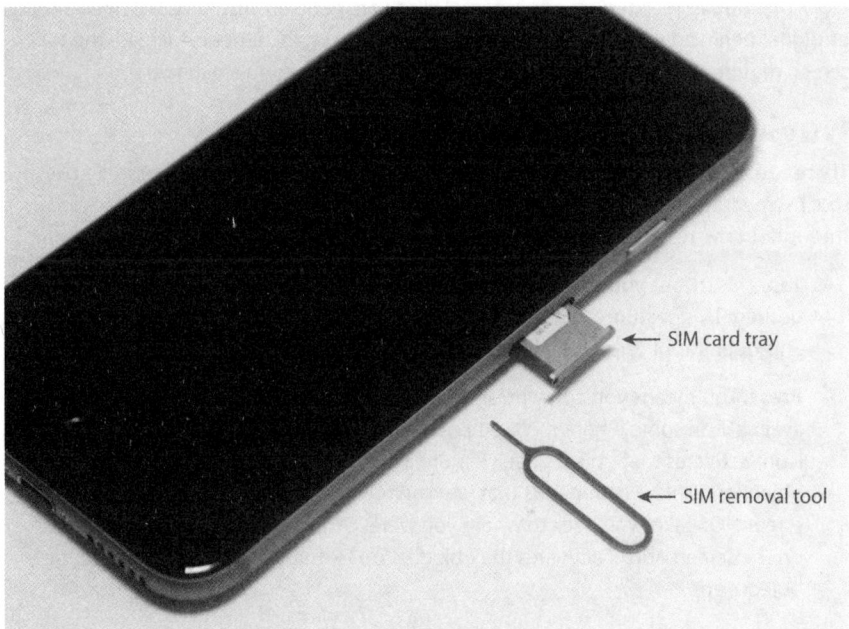

SIM card tray

SIM removal tool

1.4 Push a SIM removal tool or pin into the hole to eject the tray.

2. **Push the SIM removal tool into the hole that appears on the SIM card tray.** This tray appears just below the Side button, as shown in Figure 1.4. Insert the tool until the tray ejects.

3. **Carefully lay the SIM card into the SIM card tray.** To ensure you insert the card correctly, match the notch in one corner of the SIM card with the corresponding notch in the tray.

4. **Reinsert the SIM card tray until you feel a soft click as the tray slides into its correct position.** Your SIM card is ready to use.

Operating the Touchscreen

The most distinctive feature of the iPhone is its versatile touchscreen. You can zoom in and out, scroll through lists, drag items here and there, and even type messages. Amazingly, the touchscreen requires no external hardware to do all this. You don't need a stylus or digital pen, and you don't need to attach anything to the iPhone. Instead, the touchscreen requires just your finger (or, for some operations, a couple of fingers).

Navigating the touchscreen

There are a few maneuvers that you need to be familiar with to successfully use the touchscreen in all its glory. Take some time to try these now. I'll refer to these gestures throughout the rest of the book, so play around and make sure you understand them:

- **Tap.** This means you use your finger to quickly press and release the screen where desired. This gesture is what you use to initiate just about any action on the iPhone. This opens applications, activates options, enters text boxes, and much more.

- **Press.** This means you apply pressure to the screen to activate the 3D Touch feature available on some iPhones. A light press on a screen object (such as a Home screen icon) activates that object's Peek feature, which either gives you a sneak peek of the object or displays commands that you can run on the object. If you then release the screen, iOS takes you back to where you were. Otherwise, a slightly harder press on the screen object activates the object's Pop feature, which takes you into the object's app.

Note

3D Touch is available on iPhone models 6s, 6s Plus, 7, 7 Plus, 8, 8 Plus, X, XS, and XS Max. iPhone models XR, SE (2nd edition), 11, 11 Pro, 11 Pro Max, 12, 12 mini, 12 Pro, and 12 Pro Max all replace 3D Touch with Haptic Touch, which recognizes a long press (that is, a press that lasts a few seconds) instead of actual screen pressure.

- **Double-tap.** This is what it sounds like: two quick taps with your finger. In applications such as Photos or Safari, it zooms in on images or chunked parts of web pages. A second double-tap zooms back out.

- **Swipe and flick.** To swipe means to drag your finger across the screen. You use this technique to scroll through lists, drag items to different spots, and unlock the iPhone. Flicking is just an exaggerated swipe. This rapidly scrolls through lists. Flick your finger up and down (or sometimes left and right) on the screen and the iPhone rapidly scrolls through the list. The faster the flick, the faster the scroll. Touch the screen to stop the scrolling process.

- **Spread and pinch.** You use these techniques to zoom in on or out of the screen. To spread means to move two fingers apart, and you use it to zoom in; to pinch means to move two fingers closer together, and you use it to zoom out. This is especially useful when viewing web pages because the text is often too small to read. Spread to zoom in on the text, making it readable, and pinch to return to the full screen for easy scrolling and navigation.

Searching your iPhone

Parkinson's Law of Data pithily encapsulates an inescapable fact of digital life: "Data expands to fill the space available for storage." With each new iteration of the iPhone, the space available for storage keeps getting larger: from 4GB in the original phone to 512GB in a top-of-the-line iPhone 12. So, following Parkinson's Law, we keep adding more data to our iPhones: music, photos, videos, email messages, Safari bookmarks, and on and on.

That's cool because it means you can bring more of your digital world with you wherever you go, but there's another law that quickly comes into play; call it The Law of Digital Needles in Electronic Haystacks: "The more data you have, the harder it is to find what you need." Fortunately, iOS rides to the rescue by adding welcome search features to the iPhone.

If you use a Mac, then you probably know how indispensable the Spotlight search feature is. It's just a humble text box, but Spotlight enables you to find *anything* on your Mac in just a blink or two of an eye. It's an essential tool in this era of massive hard drives. (Windows users get much the same functionality with taskbar searches.)

The size of your iPhone storage might pale in comparison to your desktop's drive, but you can still pack an amazing amount of stuff into that tiny package, so you really need a way to search your entire iPhone, including email, contacts, calendars, bookmarks, apps, and much more. And, best of all, Spotlight on the iPhone is just as easy to use as Spotlight on the Mac:

1. **Return to any Home screen.**

2. **Swipe right to navigate the Home screens until you can't go any farther.** You should now see a screen that includes a Search box at the top.

Genius

> An often-quicker way to get to the Search box is to swipe down from the top-left corner to display the Notification Center and then swipe right.

3. **Tap in the Search box and then enter your search text.** Your iPhone immediately begins displaying items that match your text as you type, as shown in Figure 1.5.

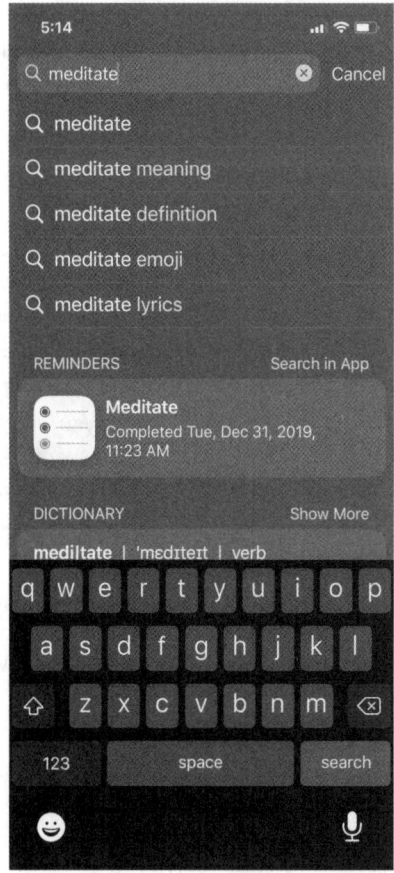

1.5 Flick down on the Home screen and then type your search text.

12

4. **Tap Search to see the complete results.** If you see the item you're looking for, tap it to open it.

Genius

Spotlight looks for a wide variety of items not only on your iPhone, but also on the Internet, iTunes, the App Store, and more. If you find you're getting too many results, you can configure Spotlight to not show results from certain apps. Tap Settings and then tap Siri & Search. In the Siri & Search screen, tap an app you want to remove from Search. Then tap the Show App in Search switch to Off and the Show Content in Search switch to Off.

Switching between running apps

Your iPhone is capable of *multitasking*, which enables you to run multiple apps at the same time. This is useful if, say, you're playing a game and an email message comes in. You can switch to the message, read it, respond to it, and then resume your game right where you left off.

So how do you switch from one app to another? It depends on your iPhone model:

- If your iPhone has a notch at the top of the screen (pointed out later in Figure 1.11), slide a finger up from the bottom edge of the screen and then pause about halfway up the screen.

- For all other iPhone models, double-press the Home button (that is, press the Home button twice in succession).

Either way, you end up at the multitasking screen, which displays thumbnail versions of your running apps. Flick left or right to bring the app thumbnail into view and then tap the app to switch to it.

Genius

To help you navigate the list of running apps, shut down any apps you won't be using for a while. Display the multitasking screen and then drag any app you want to shut down to the top of the screen.

Typing on the keyboard

You can type on your iPhone, although don't expect to pound out the prose as easily as you can on your computer. The on-screen keyboard (see Figure 1.6) is a bit too small for rapid and accurate typing, but once you get used to it (which doesn't take all that long), you'll be able to tap text fast enough to get the job done.

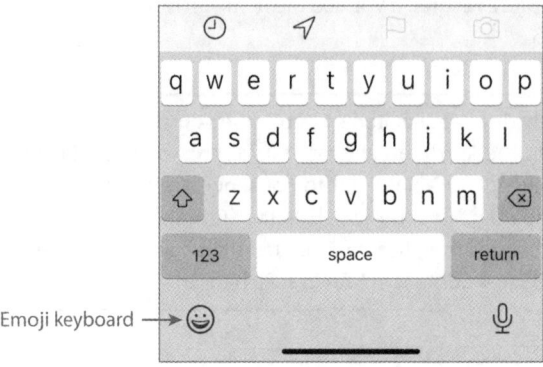

Emoji keyboard

1.6 Trust the touchscreen even though the keys may be small.

To use the keyboard, tap into an area that requires text input, and the keyboard appears automatically. Tap the keys that you want to enter. As you touch each key, a magnified version of the letter pops up. If you touch the wrong key, slide your finger over to the correct one. The keyboard does not enter a key until your finger comes off the screen.

Genius

If you find yourself trying to type on your iPhone using one hand, you might find it hard to reach all the keys unless you have an exceptionally long thumb. To make things easier on yourself, tap and hold the Emoji keyboard icon (pointed out in Figure 1.6) and then choose either the Right keyboard (if you're right-handed) or the Left keyboard (if you're left-handed). These keyboards shift the keys right and left, respectively, for easier one-handed typing.

Using special keys

The keyboard has a few specialty keys that allow you to do some tricks:

- **Shift.** This key is a little upward-pointing arrow to the left of the Z key. Tap this key once to engage Shift. The letter keys change to uppercase, and the Shift key changes to a black arrow on a white background. The next letter you type will be a capital letter, at which point the Shift key returns to normal automatically (and the letter keys return to their lowercase versions).

- **123.** Tap this key to display the numeric keyboard, which includes numbers and most punctuation marks. The key then changes to ABC. Tap ABC to return to the standard keyboard.

- **#+=.** This key appears within the numeric keyboard. Tap this key to enter yet another keyboard that contains more punctuation marks as well as a few symbols that aren't used frequently.

- **Backspace.** This key is shaped like a left-pointing arrow with an X inside it, and it appears to the right of the M key. This key deletes at three different speeds:

  - The first speed deletes in response to a single tap, which deletes just a single letter.

  - The second speed deletes in response to being held. If you hold the delete key, it begins moving backward through letters and won't stop after a single letter.

  - The third speed kicks in if you hold the delete key long enough. This deletes entire words.

- **Return.** This key moves to the next line when you're typing text. However, this key often changes names and functions, depending on what you're doing. For example, you saw earlier (see Figure 1.5) that this becomes the Search key when you invoke the Search screen.

Editing text

Everyone asks me how you're supposed to move throughout the text to edit it. The only obvious option is to delete all the way back to your error, which is impractical to say the least. The solution is in the touchscreen, which enables you to zoom in on the specific section of text you want to edit. Follow these steps:

1. **Press and hold your finger on the line you want to edit.** iPhone displays the text inside a magnifying glass, and within that text you see the cursor (you might need to angle your iPhone just so to see the cursor).

2. **Slide your finger along the line.** As you slide, the cursor moves through the text in the same direction.

3. **When the cursor is where you want to begin editing, remove your finger.**

Understanding predictive typing

As you type, the iPhone often tries to predict which word you want to use, and it displays its suggestions in a bar that appears just above the keyboard. (In earlier versions, a single suggestion appears in a little bubble underneath the current word.) This is called *predictive typing*, and the suggestions you see depend on the context of your writing.

First, the suggestion feature shows up with misspelled words. iPhone selects the text that it thinks you misspelled and then offers suggested alternatives. You have three ways to handle these suggestions:

- To accept the highlighted suggestion, tap the spacebar or any punctuation.

- To use another suggestion, tap it.

- To keep your typing as is, tap the suggestion that appears in quotation marks.

Second, as you type, the iPhone guesses what the next word might be. For example, if you type *happy*, iPhone suggests (among others) "Birthday" for the next word. If any of the suggested words is the one you want, tap it to enter the suggestion.

Selecting and copying noneditable text

How you select and then either cut or copy text depends on whether that text is editable or noneditable.

The simplest case is noneditable text, such as you get on a web page. In that scenario, when the text you want to use is on the screen, tap and hold anywhere within the text. After a second or two, your iPhone selects the text and displays blue selection handles around it, as shown in Figure 1.7. If necessary, tap and drag the selection handles to select more or less of the text and then tap Copy.

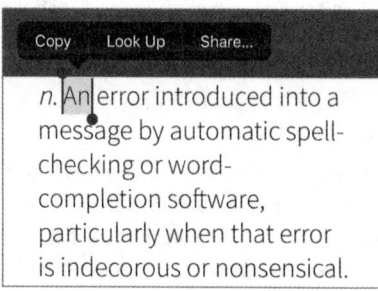

1.7 For text you can't edit, tap and hold within the text to select it and then tap Copy to copy it.

Selecting and then cutting or copying editable text

If the text is editable, such as the text in a note, an email message you're composing, or any text box, then the process is more involved, but only ever so slightly:

1. **Tap and hold anywhere within the text.** After a short pause for effect, your iPhone displays a couple of buttons above the text, as shown in Figure 1.8 (if you've previously copied some text, you'll also see a Paste button; more on this follows).

2. **Tap one of the following options:**

- **Select.** Tap this button if you want to select only some of the text. Your iPhone displays blue selection handles around the word you tapped.

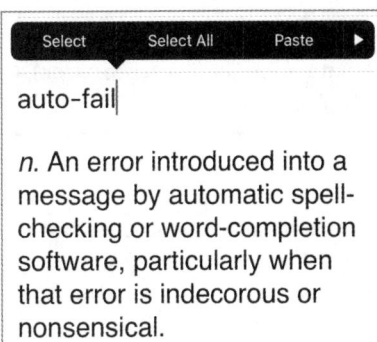

1.8 For editable text, tap and hold within the text to see these options.

- **Select All.** Tap this button if you prefer to select all the text. The iPhone displays the buttons shown in Figure 1.9; if you don't need to adjust the selection, skip to Step 4.

3. **Tap and drag the selection handles to select the text you want to work with.** The iPhone displays a new set of buttons above the text, as shown in Figure 1.9.

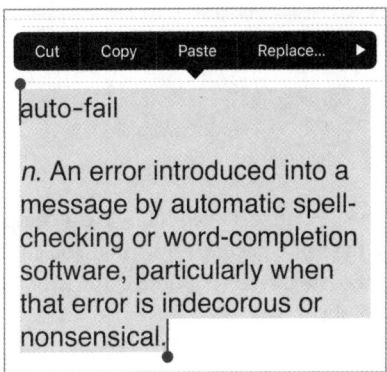

1.9 Select your text and then choose what you want to do with it.

4. **Tap the action you want iPhone to take with the text:**

- **Cut.** Tap this button to remove the text and store it in the memory of your iPhone.

- **Copy.** Tap this button to store a copy of the text in the memory of your iPhone.

17

Genius

On larger iPhones, rotate the phone into landscape mode to see an extended keyboard that includes dedicated buttons for Cut (the scissors icon), Copy (the letter A in a square), and Paste (a glue bottle).

Pasting text

With your text cut or copied and residing snugly in the memory of your iPhone, you're ready to paste the text. If you want to paste the text into a different app, open that app. Position the cursor where you want the text to appear, tap the cursor, and then tap Paste (see Figure 1.9). Your iPhone dutifully adds the cut or copied text.

Copying and pasting a photo

If you want to make a copy of a photo, such as an image shown on a web page, the process is more or less the same as copying noneditable text:

1. **Tap and hold the photo.** After a second or two, your iPhone displays a pop-up menu of image options.

2. **Tap Copy.** The iPhone copies the photo into its memory.

3. **Open the app where you want the copy of the photo to appear.**

4. **Position the cursor where you want the photo to appear and then tap the cursor.**

5. **Tap Paste.** The iPhone pastes the photo.

Undoing a paste

The Cut, Copy, and Paste commands make the iPhone feel even more like a computer. That's good, but it also means you can make the same pasting errors that you can with your regular computer. For example, you might paste the text or photo in the wrong spot, or once you've performed the paste, you might realize that you selected the wrong data.

Frustrating? Yes. A big problem? Nope! Slap your forehead lightly in exasperation and then perform one of the coolest iPhone tricks: Shake it. Your iPhone displays the options shown in Figure 1.10. Tap Undo Paste to reverse your most recent paste and then move on with your life.

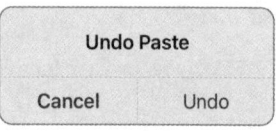

1.10 Reverse an imprudent paste by shaking the iPhone and then tapping Undo Paste.

On a larger iPhone, rotate into landscape mode and tap the Undo key (the semicircular arrow pointing to the left).

Genius

Running Your iPhone from the Control Center

As you read the rest of this book, you'll see that your iPhone is rightly called a "Swiss Army phone" because it's positively bristling with useful tools. However, unlike the easy-to-access tools in a typical Swiss Army knife, the tools on your iPhone aren't always so readily accessible. Most features and settings require several taps, which doesn't sound like much, but it can get old fast with features you use frequently.

Fortunately, iOS aims to solve that problem by offering the Control Center. This is a special screen that offers one-flick access to more than a dozen of the most useful features on your iPhone. By "one-flick access" I mean just this:

- If your iPhone has a notch at the top, flick down from the top-right edge of the screen (as pointed out in Figure 1.11).
- For all other iPhones, flick your finger up from the bottom of the screen.

This displays the Control Center, as shown in Figure 1.11, which also points out what each icon and control represents. (Depending on your iPhone model and the version of iOS it's running, you might see more or fewer icons than shown here.) Most of these features are covered elsewhere in the book, so I won't go into the details here. To hide the Control Center, tap any empty section of the Control Center screen.

You can customize the bottom row of the Control Center. Open the Settings app, tap Control Center, then add the controls you want and remove those you don't use.

Genius

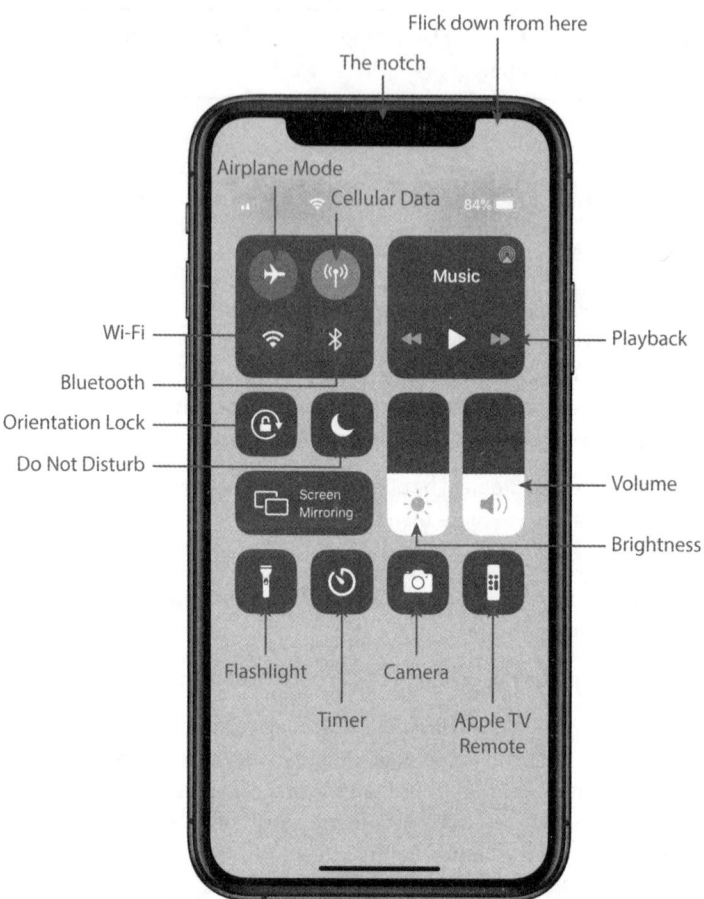

1.11 The Control Center offers "one-flick" access to some key iPhone features.

How Do I Configure My iPhone?

1 **2** **3** **4** **5** **6** **7** **8** **9** **10** **11**

The iPhone is justly famous for its stylish design and its effortless touchscreen. However, although good looks and ease of use are important for any smartphone, it's what you do with that phone that's important. The iPhone helps by offering a lot of features, but chances are those features aren't set up to suit the way you work. Maybe your most-used Home screen icons aren't at the top of the screen where they should be, or perhaps your iPhone goes to sleep too soon. This chapter shows you how to configure your iPhone to solve these and many other annoyances so the phone works the way you do.

Customizing the Home Screen

The Home screen is your starting point for all things iPhone, and what could be simpler? Just tap an icon and the app launches right away. However, you can make the Home screen even more efficient by moving your four most-used icons to the iPhone Dock (the bottom section of each Home screen) and by moving your other often-used icons to the top row or left column of the main Home screen. You can do all this by rearranging the Home screen icons as follows:

1. **Display the Home screen.**

2. **Tap and hold any Home screen icon.** iOS displays a list of actions you can perform.

3. **Tap Edit Home Screen.** iOS starts the Home screen icons a-wiggling.

4. **Tap and drag the icons into the positions you prefer.** To move an icon to a previous screen, tap and drag it to the left edge of the current screen. To move it to a later screen, tap and drag it to the right edge of the current screen. Next, wait for the new screen to appear and then drop the icon where you want it.

5. **Rearrange the existing Dock icons by dragging them left or right to change the order.**

6. **To replace a Dock icon, first tap and drag the icon off the Dock to create some space.** Then tap and drag any Home screen icon into the Dock.

7. **Stop the Home screen editing:**

   - If your iPhone has a notch at the top of the screen, tap Done, which appears to the right of the notch.

   - For all other iPhones, press the Home button.

   Your iPhone saves the new icon arrangement.

Creating an app folder

You can reduce the number of icons on the Home screens by taking advantage of a great feature called *app folders*. Just like a folder on your hard drive that can store multiple files, an app folder can store multiple app icons. This enables you to group related apps under a single icon, which not only reduces your overall Home screen clutter but can also make individual apps easier to find. Here are the steps to follow to create and populate an app folder:

1. **Navigate to the Home screen that contains at least one of the apps you want to include in your folder.**

2. **Tap and hold any Home screen icon.** iOS displays a list of actions you can perform.

3. **Tap Edit Home Screen.** The Home screen start wiggling.

4. **Tap and drag an icon that you want to include in the folder and drop it on another icon that you want to include in the same folder.** iOS creates the folder.

5. **Tap the folder.** iOS displays a text box so that you can name the folder, as shown in Figure 2.1.

6. **Tap inside the text box to edit the name and then tap Done when you finish.**

7. **Stop the Home screen editing:**

   - If your iPhone has a notch at the top of the screen, tap Done, which appears to the right of the notch.

   - For all other iPhones, press the Home button.

   Your iPhone saves your new icon arrangement.

2.1 Drop one app icon on another to create an app folder.

To launch an app, tap the folder to open it and tap the app. To work with your app folders, tap and hold any icon, tap Edit Home Screen, and then use the following techniques:

- **Add another app to a folder.** Tap and drag the app icon and drop it on the folder.

- **Rename a folder.** Tap the folder to open it and then edit the folder name.

- **Rearrange the apps within a folder.** Tap the folder to open it and then drag and drop the apps within the folder.

- **Remove an app from a folder.** Tap the folder to open it and then drag the app icon out of the folder.

Adding a web page bookmark to the Home screen

Do you have a web page that you visit all the time? If so, you can set up that page as a bookmark in the iPhone Safari browser, but there's an even faster way to access it: You can add it to the Home screen. Follow these steps to save a page as an icon on the Home screen:

1. **Use the Safari browser on your iPhone to navigate to the page you want to save.**

2. **Tap the Share icon (the arrow) at the bottom of the screen.** iPhone displays a list of actions.

3. **Tap Add to Home Screen.** iPhone prompts you to edit the web clip name.

4. **Edit the name as needed.**

5. **Tap Add.** iPhone adds the web clip to the Home screen and displays the Home screen.

Genius

If you make a bit of a mess of your Home screen or if someone else is going to be using your iPhone, you can reset the Home screen icons to their default layout. I tell you how this is done in Chapter 11.

Working with App Notifications

A lot of apps take advantage of an iOS feature called *notifications,* which enables them to send messages and other data to your iPhone. For example, the Facebook app displays an alert on your iPhone when a friend sends you a message. If an app supports notifications, then the first time you start it, your iPhone usually displays a message like the one shown in Figure 2.2, asking if you want to allow notifications for the app. Tap Allow if you're cool with that; if you're not, tap Don't Allow.

There are actually four kinds of notifications:

- **Sound.** This is a sound effect that plays when some app-related event occurs.

> **"Flickr" Would Like to Send You Notifications**
>
> Notifications may include alerts, sounds, and icon badges. These can be configured in Settings.
>
> Don't Allow   Allow

2.2 Your iPhone lets you allow or disallow notifications for an app.

- **Alert.** This is a message that pops up on your iPhone screen. You must then tap a button to dismiss the message before you can continue working with your current app.

- **Banner.** This is a message that appears at the top of the screen. Unlike an alert, a banner allows you to keep using your current app and disappears automatically after a few seconds. If you prefer to switch to the app to view the message, tap the banner.

- **Badge.** This is a small, red icon that appears in the upper-right corner of an app icon. The icon usually displays a number, which might be the number of messages you have waiting for you on the server.

Displaying the Notification Center

If you miss an alert or banner or if you see a banner but ignore it, you can still eyeball your recent notification messages by displaying the Notification Center. This is a feature that combines all your recent alerts and banners in one handy location. So, not only can you see the most recent alert, but you can also see the last few so you don't miss anything.

Even better, displaying the Notification Center is a snap: Just swipe down from the top of the screen. The Notification Center displays your recent messages sorted by app. From here, you can either tap an item to switch to that app or swipe up from the bottom of the screen to hide the Notification Center.

Handling notifications within the Notification Center

Tapping a notification opens the associated app so that you can work with the item. For example, if the notification concerns a recently received email message, you might want to tap the notification to open Mail and read or delete the message. However, for simple actions (such as viewing an email), opening the app feels like overkill. Fortunately, the Notification Center can save you a tap or two by enabling you to handle notifications directly within the Notification Center:

- **View a notification.** Either tap and hold the notification or swipe left on the notification and then tap View. Note, too, that you often get more buttons that you can tap to handle the notification. For example, if you view an email message, you see two buttons: Mark as Read and Trash (see Figure 2.3).

2.3 View a notification to reveal one or more buttons that enable you to handle the item from within the Notification Center.

- **Manage an app's notifications.** Swipe left on a notification and then tap Manage. This brings up the following actions:

  - **Deliver Quietly.** Configures the app to deliver notifications without playing a sound or displaying a banner or badge.

  - **Turn Off.** Stops all notifications from the app.

  - **Settings.** Takes you to the app's notification settings, which I describe in the next section.

- **Clear one or more notifications.** Swipe left on the notification and then tap Clear. If the notifications are organized as a group in Notification Center, swipe left on the group and then tap Clear All.

Customizing notifications

For each app, your iPhone lets you toggle individual notification types (sounds, alerts, and badges), switch between banner and alert messages, or remove an app from the Notification Center altogether. You can also configure app notifications to appear in the Lock screen (with the Lock screen displayed, swipe down from the top of the screen to see the Notification Center). This is handy because you can see your notifications without having to unlock your iPhone.

Here's how to configure app notifications:

1. **On the Home screen, tap Settings.** The Settings app appears.

2. **Tap Notifications.** The Notifications screen appears.

3. **Tap the app you want to customize.** The app notification settings appear. Figure 2.4 shows the settings for the Reminders app. Note that not all apps support all possible settings.

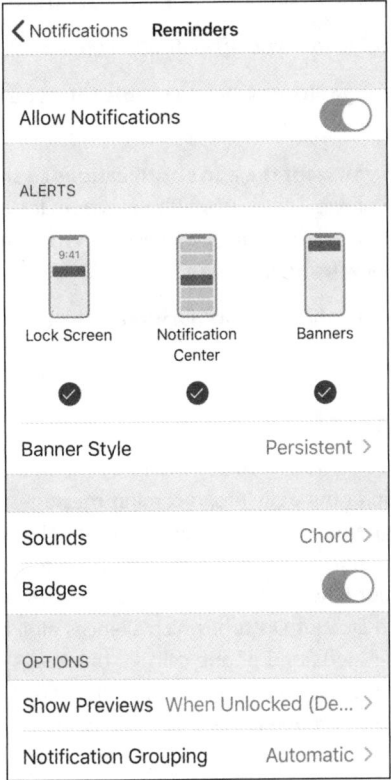

2.4 Use each app's notification settings to control notifications on your iPhone.

4. **If you prefer not to receive notifications from the app, tap the Allow Notifications switch to Off and then skip the rest of these steps.**

5. **In the Alerts section, tap the styles you prefer for message notifications.** Tap to toggle Lock Screen, Notification Center, or Banners.

6. **Tap Banner Style and then select the banner type you prefer for the app.** Tap Temporary to have each banner disappear automatically after a few seconds; tap Persistent to have each banner stay on-screen until you dismiss it.

7. **If the app supports sound notifications, you'll see one of the following setting types:**

   ◉ **Sounds menu.** Tap this to select a sound to play or tap None to play no sound.

   ◉ **Sounds switch.** Tap this switch to toggle this type of notification on or off.

8. **If the app supports badges, use the Badges Icon switch to toggle this type of notification on or off.**

9. **Tap Show Previews and choose when you want the app's notifications to show a preview.** Always means you can see a preview when your iPhone is both locked and unlocked, When Unlocked means you can see a preview only when your phone isn't locked, and Never disables the preview feature.

10. **Tap Notification Grouping to choose how the app's notifications are grouped in the Notification Center.**

Configuring Do Not Disturb settings

The Notification Center is a truly useful tool that helps you see what's going on in your world at a glance and gives you a heads-up about activities, incoming messages, app happenings, and more. The Notification Center is a great innovation, but it's also a distracting one with its banners, alerts, and sounds. If you're in a meeting, at a movie, or going to sleep, you certainly don't want your iPhone disturbing the peace. iOS solves this conundrum by offering a feature called Do Not Disturb, which silences all iPhone distractions — including Notification Center alerts and phone calls — but keeps your iPhone online so that it can continue to receive data. That way, when you're ready to get back to the action, all your new data is already on your iPhone, so you can get back up to speed quickly.

You can get even more out of Do Not Disturb by configuring it to suit the way you work. Here are the steps to follow:

1. **Tap Settings to open the Settings app.**

2. **Tap Do Not Disturb.** The Do Not Disturb screen appears.

3. **To set a time to automatically activate and deactivate Do Not Disturb, tap the Scheduled switch to On.** You then use the From controls to set the start time and use the To controls to set the end time.

4. **If you want Do Not Disturb to handle calls and notifications normally (that is, nonsilently) when your iPhone is unlocked, tap the Only While iPhone Is Locked option.**

5. **If you want to allow certain calls even when Do Not Disturb is activated, tap Allow Calls From and then tap who you want to get through: Everyone, No One, Favorites (that is, anyone in the Phone app's Favorites list), or a particular contact group.**

6. **If you want Do Not Disturb to allow a call through when the same person calls twice within 3 minutes, leave the Repeated Calls switch in the On position.** If you don't want to allow this exception, tap the Repeated Calls switch to Off.

Note

To turn on Do Not Disturb outside of the scheduled time, tap Settings, tap Do Not Disturb, and then tap the Do Not Disturb switch to On. Alternatively, open the Control Center and tap Do Not Disturb (pointed out in Figure 1.11).

Genius

Do Not Disturb is perfect for when you're driving because if there was ever a time your iPhone shouldn't disturb you, it's when you're behind the wheel. To make sure this works, tap Activate in the Do Not Disturb While Driving section and then tap Automatically (which means iOS activates Do Not Disturb when it detects that your car is moving). If your iPhone connects to Bluetooth in the car, you could alternatively tap the When Connected to Car Bluetooth option.

More Useful iPhone Configuration Techniques

You've seen quite a few handy iPhone customization tricks so far, but you're not done yet — not by a long shot. The next few sections take you through a few more heartwarmingly useful iPhone customization techniques.

Changing the name of your iPhone

Feel free to rename your iPhone for the sake of giving it a cool or snappy name if the mood strikes. Here's how:

1. **On the iPhone Home screen, tap Settings.** The Settings screen appears.

2. **Tap General.** The General settings appear.

3. **Tap About.** The About page appears.

4. **Tap Name.** The Settings app displays a text box with the current name of your iPhone.

5. **Edit the name as you see fit.**

Turning sounds on and off

Your iPhone is often a noisy little thing that makes all manner of rings, beeps, and boops, seemingly at the slightest provocation. None of this may bother you when you're on your own, but if you're in a meeting, at a movie, or anywhere else where extraneous sounds are unwelcome, you might want to turn off some (or all) of the iPhone sound effects. You can control exactly which sounds your iPhone utters by following these steps:

1. **On the Home screen, tap Settings.** The Settings app appears.

2. **Tap Sounds & Haptics.** The Sounds & Haptics screen appears.

3. **The two switches in the Vibrate section determine whether your iPhone vibrates when the phone rings or is in Silent Mode.** Vibrating probably isn't all that important in Ring Mode, so feel free to change this setting to Off. The exception is if you reduce and/or lock the ringer volume (see Steps 4 and 5), in which case setting Vibrate on Ring to On might help you notice an incoming call. Vibrating in Silent Mode is a good idea, so On is a good choice for the Vibrate on Silent setting.

4. **In the Ringer and Alerts section, drag the volume slider to set the volume of the ringtone that plays when a call comes in.**

5. **To lock the ringer volume, tap the Change with Buttons switch to Off.** This means that pressing the volume buttons on the side of the iPhone will have no effect on the ringer volume.

Genius

Locking the ringer volume is a good idea because it prevents one of the major iPhone frustrations: missing a call because the ringer volume has been muted accidentally (for example, by your iPhone getting jostled in a purse or pocket).

6. **To set a different default ringtone, tap Ringtone to open the Ringtone screen.** Tap the ringtone you want to use (iPhone plays a preview) and then tap Back to return to the Sounds screen.

7. **For each of the other events in the list (from Text Tone to AirDrop), tap the event and then tap the sound you want to hear.** You can also tap None to turn off the event sound.

8. **To turn off the sound that your iPhone makes each time you tap a key on the virtual keyboard, tap the Keyboard Clicks switch to Off.**

9. **To turn off the sound that your iPhone makes when you lock and unlock it, tap the Lock Sound switch to Off.**

Genius

One of the truly annoying iPhone sound effects is the clicking sound made by each key when using the on-screen keyboard. If it doesn't make you batty after 5 minutes, it will certainly drive anyone within earshot to thoughts of violence. So, I strongly recommend tapping the Keyboard Clicks setting to Off. There, that's better.

Customizing the keyboard

Did you know that the keyboard changes depending on the app you use? For example, the regular keyboard features a spacebar at the bottom. However, if you're entering an email address in the Mail app, the keyboard that appears offers a smaller spacebar and uses the extra space to show an at sign (@) key and a period (.) key, two characters that are part of any email address. Nice! Here are some other nice innovations you get with the iPhone keyboard:

- **Auto-Capitalization.** If you type a punctuation mark that indicates the end of a sentence — for example, a period (.), a question mark (?), or an exclamation mark (!) — or if you press Return to start a new paragraph, the iPhone automatically activates the Shift key, because it assumes you're starting a new sentence.

- **Double-tapping the spacebar.** This activates a keyboard shortcut: Instead of entering two spaces, the iPhone automatically enters a period (.) followed by a space. This is a welcome bit of efficiency because otherwise you'd have to tap the Number key (123) to display the numbers and punctuation marks, tap the period (.), and then tap the spacebar.

Genius

> Typing a number or punctuation mark normally requires three taps: tapping Number (123), tapping the number or symbol, and then tapping ABC. Here's a faster way: Use one finger to tap and hold the Number key to open the numeric keyboard, use a second finger to tap the number or punctuation symbol you want, and then release the Number key. This types the number or symbol and returns you to the regular keyboard.

- **Auto-Correction.** For many people, one of the keys to quick iPhone typing is to clear the mind and just tap away without worrying about accuracy. In many cases, you'll actually be rather amazed at how accurate this willy-nilly approach can be. Why does it work? The secret is the Auto-Correction feature on your iPhone, which eyeballs what you're typing and automatically corrects any errors. For example, if you tap *hte,* your iPhone automatically corrects this to *the.* Your iPhone displays the suggested correction before you complete the word (say, by tapping a space or a comma), and you can reject the suggestion by tapping the typed text that appears with quotation marks in the predictive typing bar. If you find you never use the predictive suggestions, you can turn them off to save a bit of screen real estate.

- **Caps Lock.** One thing the iPhone keyboard doesn't seem to have is a Caps Lock feature that, when activated, enables you to type all-uppercase letters. To do this, you need to tap and hold the Shift key and then use a different finger to tap the uppercase letters. However, the iPhone actually does have a Caps Lock feature: Double-tap Shift to turn Caps Lock on (which is indicated on the Shift key with a horizontal bar under the arrow), then tap Shift to turn Caps Lock off.

- **Slide to Type.** If you're *really* in a hurry, you might resent the split second that elapses between the tap of each key. To shave even that small amount of time off your typing chores, you can use the Slide to Type feature, where instead of tapping each key individually, you quickly slide your finger from one letter to the next, only lifting your finger when you complete each word. (Yep, iOS adds a space automatically.) It takes a bit of getting used to, but it can make entering text crazy-fast.

- **Character preview.** This feature displays a pop-up version of each character as you tap it. This is great for iPhone keyboard rookies because it helps them be sure they're typing accurately, but veterans often find it distracting. Some even complain that it's a security risk because the letters pop up even when you're typing a password! That might be why Apple chooses to turn off character preview by default, but you can turn it on if you miss it.

To change the settings for any of these keyboard features, follow these steps:

1. **On the Home screen, tap Settings.** The Settings app appears.

2. **Tap General.** The General screen appears.

3. **Tap Keyboard.** The Keyboard screen appears.

4. **Use the switches — including Auto-Capitalization, Auto-Correction, Enable Caps Lock, Predictive, Slide to Type, Character Preview, and "." Shortcut — to toggle keyboard features off and on as you prefer.**

Setting up Apple Pay

Prior to 2020, paying for things by waving your phone at a contactless reader was convenient, but not essential. Then the Great Pandemic of 2020 came along, and suddenly the virtues of going "contactless" became glaringly obvious. If you'd like to use your iPhone to pay for stuff without having to press any buttons or insert a payment card, then you need to configure Apply Pay on your device. Here's what you do:

1. **Open the Settings app.**

2. **Tap Wallet & Apple Pay.** The Wallet & Apple Pay screen appears.

3. **Tap Add Card.**

4. **Tap Continue.** iOS displays a camera frame.

5. **Place your payment card on a flat surface and then position the camera frame so that the card fills the frame.** You might have to hover the frame over the card for a few seconds before iOS recognizes it and displays the Card Details screen.

6. **Double-check that your name and card number are accurate; then tap Next.** If either or both your name and card number contain an error, edit as needed and then tap Next.

7. **Select the card's expiration month and year (if needed; these should already be entered for you), type the card's three-digit security code, and then tap Next.** iOS displays some terms and conditions.

8. **Read the terms and conditions (I jest, of course) and then tap Agree.**

9. **If your card requires verification, tap the method you prefer to use (such as Text Message), tap Next, and then enter the verification code when you receive it.** Note that if your verification device is the same iPhone as the one you're using, iOS will enter the verification code for you automatically.

10. **The next steps depend on whether you're adding your first card or a subsequent card:**

    - **You're adding your first payment card.** iOS adds the payment card to your iPhone's digital wallet and then shows a screen with instructions on using Apple Pay. Tap Continue. iOS returns you to the Wallet & Apple Pay screen.

    - **You're adding a subsequent payment card.** iOS asks if you want this new card to be the default for payments. If so, tap Use as Default Card; otherwise, tap Not Now. iOS adds the payment card to your iPhone's digital wallet and then returns you to the Wallet & Apple Pay screen.

11. **If you want to add more payment cards, repeat Steps 3 through 10.**

You might be wondering how you pay for something when you have multiple payment cards. Here's how:

- To pay with the default card, double-press either the Side button (if your iPhone has Face ID) or the Home button, verify that it's you (with Face ID, Touch ID, or a passcode), and then hold the phone near the contactless reader until the transaction is complete.

- To pay with another card, double-press either the Side button (if your iPhone has Face ID) or the Home button and then verify that it's you (with Face ID, Touch ID, or a passcode). You now see a screen similar to the one shown in Figure 2.5, which shows your default card at the top and your other cards at the bottom. Tap the bottom cards, tap the card you want to use, and then hold the phone near the contactless reader until the transaction is complete.

Note

Face ID obviously won't work if you're wearing a mask! In that case, iOS enables you to use a secondary verification method, such as your passcode.

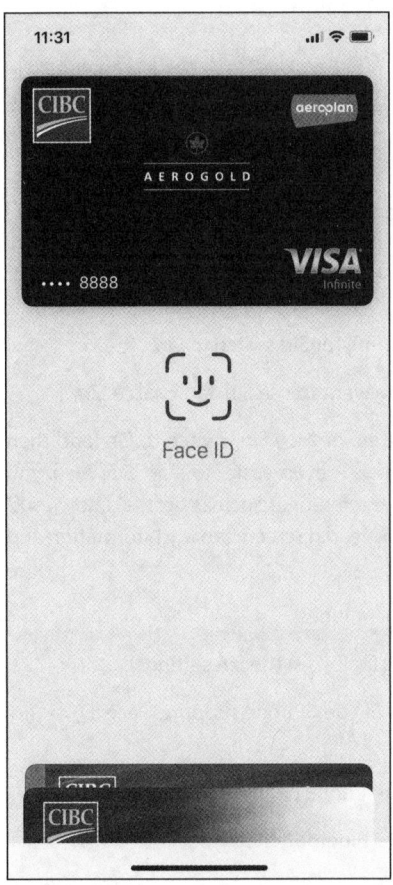

2.5 The wallet shows your default card at the top and your other cards at the bottom.

Genius

To specify a different payment card as the default, follow Steps 1 and 2 to open the Wallet & Apple Pay screen, tap Default Card, and then tap the card you prefer to use as the default. Alternatively, open the Wallet app and then tap and drag the card you want to use as the default to the front of the stack.

Configuring Siri

You can make things happen on your iPhone via voice commands by using the Siri app, which not only lets you launch apps, but also gives you voice control over web searching, appointments, contacts, reminders, map navigation, text messages, notes, and much more.

First, make sure that Siri is activated by tapping Settings on the Home screen, tapping Siri & Search, and then doing one of the following:

- If your iPhone supports Face ID, tap the Press Side Button for Siri switch to On.

- For all other iPhone models, tap the Press Home for Siri switch to On.

Either way, when iOS asks you to confirm that you want to use Siri, tap Enable Siri.

While you're here, you might want to tap the Listen for "Hey Siri" switch to On (and then run through a brief setup procedure), which makes it even easier to start Siri. Also, you should tell Siri who you are so that when you use references such as "home" and "work," Siri knows what you're talking about. On the Siri & Search screen, tap My Information and then tap your item in the Contacts list.

You crank up Siri by using any of the following techniques:

- Saying "Hey Siri" (assuming you enabled this feature in the Siri settings).

- Pressing and holding either the Side button (if your iPhone supports Face ID) or the Home button.

- Pressing and holding the Mic button on your iPhone headphones.

- Pressing and holding the Mic equivalent on a Bluetooth headset.

Siri is often easier to use if you define relationships within it. So, for example, instead of saying "Call Sandy Evans," you can simply say "Call mom." You can define relationships in two ways:

- **Within the Contacts app.** Open the Contacts app, tap your contact item, tap Edit, tap Add Related Name, and then tap the relationship you want to use. Tap the blue More icon to open the All Contacts list and then tap the person you want to add to the field.

- **Within Siri.** Say "*Name* is my *relationship*," where *Name* is the person's name as given in your Contacts list, and *relationship* is the connection, such as *wife, husband, spouse, partner, brother, sister, mother,* or *father.* When Siri asks you to confirm, say "Yes."

Controlling your privacy

Third-party apps occasionally request permission to use the data from another app. For example, an app might need access to your contacts, your calendars, your photos, or your Twitter and Facebook accounts. You can always deny these requests, of course, but if you've allowed access to an app in the past, you might later change your mind and decide you'd prefer to revoke that access. Fortunately, iOS offers a Privacy feature that enables you to control which apps have access to your data. Here's how it works:

1. **On the Home screen, tap Settings to open the Settings app.**

2. **Tap Privacy.** The Privacy screen appears.

3. **Tap the app or feature for which you want to control access.** Your iPhone displays a list of third-party apps that have requested access to the app or feature.

4. **To revoke a third-party app's access to the app or feature, tap its switch to Off.**

Protecting Your iPhone

These days, an iPhone is much more than just a phone. You use it to surf the web, send and receive email and text messages, manage your contacts and schedules, find your way in the world, and much more. This is handy, for sure, but it also means that your iPhone is jammed with tons of information about you. Even though you might not store the nuclear launch codes on your iPhone, chances are what is on it is pretty important to you. Therefore, you should take steps to protect your iPhone, and that's what the next few sections are all about.

Locking your iPhone with a passcode

If you have sensitive or confidential information on your phone or if you want to avoid digital joyrides that run up massive roaming or data charges, you need to lock your iPhone. You do that by specifying a passcode that must be entered before anyone can use the iPhone. The default in iOS is a six-digit passcode, but you can change that either to a simple four-digit passcode or to a custom code that is longer and more complex and uses any combination of numbers, letters, and symbols. Follow these steps to set up your passcode:

1. **On the Home screen, tap Settings.** The Settings app appears.

2. **Tap Face ID & Passcode.** If your iPhone supports Touch ID, tap Touch ID & Passcode instead.

3. **Tap Turn Passcode On.** The Set Passcode screen appears.

4. **If you prefer to use something other than a six-digit passcode, tap Passcode Options and then tap the type of passcode you want to use.**

5. **Tap your passcode.** For security, the characters appear in the passcode box as dots.

6. **If you're entering a custom passcode, tap Next.** Your iPhone prompts you to reenter the passcode.

7. **Tap your passcode again.**

8. **If you're entering a custom passcode, tap Done.**

Caution

You really, really need to remember your iPhone passcode. If you forget it, you're locked out of your own phone. The only way to get back in is to restore the data and settings to your iPhone from an existing backup (as described in Chapter 11).

Caution

Auto-Lock is a crucial feature if you've protected your iPhone with a passcode lock because if your iPhone never sleeps, it never locks, either. To make sure your iPhone sleeps automatically, open the Settings app, tap Display & Brightness, tap Auto-Lock, and then tap the interval you want to use.

Unlocking your iPhone biometrically

Protecting your iPhone with a passcode is just good sense in this age of so-called "iCrime," where thieves routinely go "Apple picking" by snatching iPhones and other Apple devices from the unwary. With a passcode acting as a digital barrier between the crook and your iPhone, at least your personal data is safe from prying eyes. Yes, a passcode is a smart safety precaution, but it's not always a convenient one. Having to tap that four-character (or more) code many times during the day adds a small but nevertheless unwelcome annoyance to using the iPhone.

As an extra (and more convenient) layer of security, you can configure your iPhone with a biometric lock, which means you can only unlock the device using either your face or a fingerprint:

● If your iPhone supports Face ID, open the Settings app, tap Face ID & Passcode, tap Set Up Face ID, and then follow the instructions.

- If your iPhone supports Touch ID, open the Settings app, tap Touch ID & Passcode, tap Set Up Face ID, and then follow the instructions. Note that you can set up multiple fingerprints for Touch ID.

Configuring parental controls

If your children have access to your iPhone or if they have iPhones of their own, then you might be a bit worried about some of the content they might be exposed to on the web, on YouTube, or in other apps. Similarly, you might not want them installing apps or giving away their current location.

For all those and similar parental worries, you can sleep better at night by activating the Screen Time app's parental controls on your iPhone. These controls restrict the content and activities that kids can see and do. Here's how to set them up:

1. **On the Home screen, tap Settings.** The Settings app appears.

2. **Tap Screen Time.** The Screen Time settings appear.

3. **Tap Turn On Screen Time and then tap Continue.** iOS asks if you're configuring Screen Time for yourself or for a child.

4. **Tap This is My Child's iPhone.** The Downtime screen appears.

5. **Set the start and end times for when your child is not allowed to use the phone without your permission and then tap Set Downtime.** The App Limits screen appears.

6. **Select each of the app categories you want to limit (or, select All Apps and Categories to cover everything), tap Set, select the maximum amount of time your child is allowed for the selected categories, and then tap Set App Limit.** The Content & Privacy screen appears.

7. **Tap Continue.** iOS prompts you to enter a Screen Time passcode.

8. **Tap a passcode (twice).** iOS asks for an Apple ID to use to recover your Screen Time passcode.

9. **Type your Apple ID email and password and then tap OK.**

Locating and protecting a lost iPhone

If there's a downside to using a smartphone (particularly one as smart as the iPhone), it's that you end up with a pretty large chunk of your life on that phone. Initially, that may sound like a good thing, but if you happen to lose your phone, you've also lost that chunk of your life. Plus, assuming you haven't configured your iPhone with a passcode lock, as described earlier, you've opened a gaping privacy hole because anyone can now delve into your data. I'm sure you'd love to find your iPhone because it's expensive and there's just something creepy about the thought of some stranger flicking through your stuff.

You can locate a lost iPhone using an app called Find My. (You can also use this feature through your iCloud account, if you have one.) Find My uses the GPS sensor embedded inside your iPhone to locate the device. You can also use Find My to play a sound on your iPhone, remotely lock it and send a message, or, in a real pinch, remotely delete your data. The next few sections provide the details.

Note

You might think that a fatal flaw with Find My iPhone is that someone who has your iPhone can easily turn off the feature and disable it. Fortunately, that's not the case because your iPhone comes with a feature called Activation Lock, which means that a person can turn off Find My iPhone only by entering your Apple ID password.

Activating Find My iPhone

Find My works by looking for a particular signal that your iPhone beams out into the ether. This signal is turned off by default, so you need to turn it on if you ever plan to use Find My. Here are the steps to follow:

1. **Add your iCloud account, if you haven't done so already, as described in Chapter 10.** When you add the account, be sure to tap OK when iCloud asks if it can use your location.

2. **On the Home screen, tap Settings.** The Settings app appears.

3. **Tap your name at the top of the Settings screen.** Your Apple ID settings appear.

4. **Tap Find My.** The Find My screen appears.

5. **Tap Find My iPhone and then tap the Find My iPhone switch to On.**

Genius

Your lost iPhone might just be somewhere no one can find it. In that case, the danger is that the iPhone battery will die before you have a chance to locate it using Find My. To make this less likely, be sure to activate the Send Last Location switch. This configures your iPhone to send you the phone's last known location as soon as it detects that its battery is nearly done.

With Find My iPhone now active on your iPhone, you can use the Find My app or iCloud to locate it at any time. The next two sections show you how to do this.

Locating your iPhone using the Find My app

Follow these steps to see your lost iPhone on a map using the Find My app:

1. **On an iPhone, iPad, or iPod touch that has the Find My app installed, tap the app to launch it.**

2. **Tap Devices.** Find My displays a list of devices.

3. **Tap your lost iPhone.** The Find My app locates the iPhone on a map.

Locating your iPhone using iCloud

Follow these steps to see your lost iPhone on a map using iCloud:

1. **Log in to your iCloud account.**

2. **Click Find iPhone and, if prompted, enter your iCloud password.** The iCloud Find My iPhone application appears.

3. **Click All Devices.** iCloud displays a list of your devices.

4. **Click your iPhone in the list.** iCloud locates your iPhone on a map.

Getting an email message when your iPhone comes online

Find My iPhone is useful only if you can, you know, *find* your iPhone. That won't happen if your iPhone is powered off or not connected to the Internet. You could keep refreshing the list of devices, but it could be hours before your iPhone comes online. To avoid a constant vigil, you can tell Find My to send an email message to your iCloud account as soon as your iPhone comes online:

1. **Display the My Devices list.**

2. **Tap or click your iPhone in the devices list.** Find My displays information about your iPhone.

3. **If Find My iPhone has no location data for your iPhone, select Notify When Found.**

Playing a sound on your iPhone

If you misplace your phone, the first thing you should try is calling your number using another phone so you can (hopefully!) hear it ringing. That might not work, however, because your phone might have Ring/Silent switched to Silent Mode, it might be in Airplane Mode, or you might not have another phone handy. In any case, you only get so many rings before the call goes to voicemail, so unless you locate your phone right away, calling your number isn't always the best solution.

Your next step when looking for a lost iPhone is to use Find My to play a sound on your phone. This sound plays even if your iPhone is in Silent Mode or Airplane Mode, and it plays loudly even if your iPhone has its volume turned down or muted. Here's how it works:

1. **Display the My Devices list.**

2. **Tap or click your iPhone in the list.** Find My locates your iPhone on a map.

3. **Tap or click Play Sound.** Find My iPhone begins playing the sound on your iPhone, and it also displays an alert message.

4. **When you find your iPhone (fingers crossed), tap the alert to silence the sound.**

Locking the data on your lost iPhone

If you can't find your iPhone right away by playing a sound, your next step should be to ensure that some other person who finds the phone can't rummage around in your stuff. You do that by putting your iPhone into Lost Mode, which remotely locks the iPhone using the passcode that you set earlier. (Sorry, if you didn't protect your iPhone with a passcode, you can't remotely lock your phone.) You can also provide a phone number where you can be reached and send a message for whoever finds your iPhone. Follow these steps to put your iPhone into Lost Mode:

1. **Display the My Devices list.**

2. **Tap or click your iPhone in the list.** The app locates your iPhone on a map.

3. **Enable Lost Mode:**

   ◉ **Find My app.** In the Mark As Lost section, tap Activate and then tap Continue.

   ◉ **iCloud.** Click Lost Mode.

4. **Enter a passcode (twice) to lock the iPhone.** You're prompted to enter a phone number where you can be reached.

5. **Type your phone number and then tap or click Next.** You're prompted to type a message that will appear on the iPhone along with the phone number.

6. **Type the message and then either tap Activate or click Done.** Find My iPhone remotely locks the iPhone and displays the message.

Deleting the data on your lost iPhone

If you can't get the other person to return your iPhone and it contains sensitive or confidential data — or just that big chunk of your life I mentioned earlier — you can use the Find My app or the iCloud Find My iPhone feature to take the drastic step of remotely wiping all the data from your iPhone. Here's what you do:

1. **Display the My Devices list.**

2. **Tap or click your iPhone in the list.** The app locates your iPhone on a map.

3. **Initiate the erase procedure:**

   - **Find My app.** Tap Erase This Device and then tap Continue.

   - **iCloud.** Click Erase iPhone, click Erase, type your Apple password, and then click Next.

   The app asks you to enter an optional phone number where you can be reached, which will appear on the iPhone after it has been erased.

4. **Type your phone number and then select Next.** The app prompts you to type a message that will appear on the iPhone along with the phone number, after it has been erased.

5. **Type the message and then either tap Erase or click Done.** The app remotely wipes all data from the iPhone.

How Do I Connect My iPhone to a Network?

As a standalone device, your iPhone works just fine, thank you, because you can make calls, listen to music, take pictures, record and edit video, work with your contacts and calendars, take notes, play games, and much more. But your iPhone was made to connect: to surf the web, exchange email and text messages, watch YouTube videos, navigate with maps, and on and on. To do all that, your iPhone must first connect to a network, and that's what this chapter is all about. I show you how to make, monitor, and control network connections; set up your iPhone as an Internet hub; and more.

Connecting to a Wi-Fi Network

Connections to a cellular network are automatic and occur behind the scenes. As soon as you switch on your iPhone, it checks for an LTE or 5G signal. If it finds one, it connects to the network and displays the LTE or 5G icon in the status bar, as well as the connection strength (the more bars, the better). If your current area doesn't do either LTE or 5G, your iPhone tries to connect to the slower 3G network. If that works, you see the 3G icon in the status bar and the connection strength. If there's no 3G network in sight, your iPhone tries to connect to a slower EDGE network instead. If that works, you see the E icon in the status bar (plus the usual signal strength bars). If none of that works, you see No Signal, so you might as well go home.

Making your first connection

Things aren't automatic when it comes to Wi-Fi connections, at least not at first. To see the list of available networks, you have two options:

- Display the Control Center, long press anywhere in the section that includes the Wi-Fi icon, and then tap and hold the Wi-Fi icon.

- Open the Settings app and then tap Wi-Fi.

Whichever method you use, you see a list of nearby networks, as shown in Figure 3.1.

3.1 If you're just starting out on the Wi-Fi trail, get your iPhone to display a list of nearby networks.

For each network, you get three tidbits of data:

- **Network name.** This is the name that the administrator has assigned to the network. If you're in a coffee shop or similar public hotspot and you want to use that network, look for the name of the shop (or a variation on the name).

- **Password-protection.** If a Wi-Fi network displays a lock icon, it means that it's protected by a password, and you need that password to make the connection.

- **Signal strength.** This icon gives you a rough idea of how strong the wireless signals are. The stronger the signal (the more bars you see, the better the signal), the more likely you are to get a fast and reliable connection.

Follow these steps to connect to one of these Wi-Fi networks:

1. **Tap the network you want to use.** If the network is protected by a password, your iPhone prompts you to enter it.

2. **Type the password.**

Caution

Because the password box shows dots instead of the actual text for added security, this is no place to demonstrate your iPhone speed-typing prowess. Keep it slow and steady and note that the iPhone displays the actual character you type for about a second before changing it to a dot, so you can check your typing as you go.

3. **Tap Join.** The iPhone connects to the network and adds the Wi-Fi network signal strength icon to the status bar.

To connect to a commercial Wi-Fi operation — such as those you find in airports, hotels, and convention centers — you almost always have to take one more step. Usually, the network prompts you for your name and credit card data so you can be charged for accessing the network. If you're not prompted right away, you will be as soon as you try to access a web site or check your email. Enter your information and then enjoy the Internet in all its (expensive) Wi-Fi glory.

Showing available Wi-Fi networks automatically

If you're moving around town, having to constantly display the list of available Wi-Fi networks manually can become a pain. To ease that pain, you can configure your iPhone to display the list automatically.

Here's how:

1. **On the Home screen, tap Settings.** The Settings app appears.

2. **Tap Wi-Fi.** iPhone opens the Wi-Fi Networks screen.

3. **Tap Ask to Join Networks.** The Ask to Join Networks screen appears.

4. **Tap Ask.**

Genius

Rather than activating the Ask option in the Ask to Join Networks screen, an alternative is the Notify option. When you activate Notify, iOS only looks for nearby networks that are popular (that is, being accessed by many people). If iOS finds such a network, it displays a notification to let you know, and you can then tap Join to access the network.

Now, as soon as you try to access something on the Internet — a web site, your email, a map, or whatever — your iPhone scours the surrounding airwaves for Wi-Fi network signals. If you've never connected to a Wi-Fi network or if you're in an area that doesn't have any Wi-Fi networks that you've used in the past, you see the list of nearby wireless networks automatically. Sweet.

Connecting to known networks

Your iPhone remembers any Wi-Fi network to which you connect. So, if the network is one that you use all the time — for example, your home or office — your iPhone makes the connection without so much as a peep as soon as that network comes within range. Thanks!

Connecting to a hidden Wi-Fi network

Each Wi-Fi network has a network name — often called the Service Set Identifier, or SSID — that identifies the network to Wi-Fi–friendly devices, such as your iPhone. By default, most Wi-Fi networks broadcast the network name so that you can see it and connect to it. However, some Wi-Fi networks disable network name broadcasting as a security precaution. The idea here is that if an unauthorized user can't see the network, he or she can't attempt to connect to it. (However, some devices can still pick up the network name when authorized computers connect to it, so this is not a foolproof security measure.)

You can still connect to a hidden Wi-Fi network by entering the connection settings by hand. You need to know the network name, its security and encryption types, and the network password. Here are the steps to follow:

1. **On the Home screen, tap Settings to open the Settings app.**

2. **Tap Wi-Fi.** You see the Wi-Fi Networks screen.

3. **In the list of networks, tap Other.** Your iPhone displays the Other Network screen, as shown in Figure 3.2.

4. **Type the network name in the Name text box.**

5. **Tap Security to open the Security screen.**

6. **Tap the type of security the Wi-Fi network uses: None, WEP, WPA, WPA2/ WPA3, WPA3, WPA Enterprise, WPA2 Enterprise, or WPA3 Enterprise.** If you're not sure, most secure networks use WPA2/WPA3.

Enter network information		
Cancel	**Other Network**	Join
Name	Network Name	
Security		WPA2/WPA3 >
Password		

3.2 Use the Other Network screen to connect to a hidden Wi-Fi network.

7. **Tap Back to return to the Other Network screen.** If you chose a network security type other than None, your iPhone prompts you to type the password.

8. **Type the password in the Password text box.**

9. **Tap Join.** The iPhone connects to the network and adds the Wi-Fi network signal strength icon to the status bar.

Sending a file from your Mac to your iPhone

If your Mac is running OS X Yosemite or later and your Mac and iPhone are connected to the same Wi-Fi network, you can use a tool called AirDrop to send a file directly from your Mac to your phone. Here's how it works:

1. **On your Mac, open Finder and click AirDrop in the sidebar.** You can also click Go → AirDrop or press cmd+Shift+R. You should see an icon for your iPhone in the AirDrop window.

Note If you don't see your iPhone, make sure it has AirDrop turned on. Open the Settings app, tap General, tap AirDrop, and then tap Contacts Only. If you still don't see your iPhone on your Mac, tap Everyone instead. If you tap Everyone, then for security reasons you should tap Contacts Only after the transfer is complete. For even better security, tap Receiving Off; you can always turn AirDrop back on when you need it.

2. **Open a second Finder window (click File → New Finder Window) and use it to locate the file you want to send to your iPhone.**

3. **Drag the file from the Finder window and drop it on your iPhone icon in the AirDrop window.** If the sender is in your Contacts, your iPhone either opens the file or asks you to select an app to open the file; if the sender isn't in your Contacts, your iPhone asks you to confirm the transfer by tapping Accept.

4. **If your iPhone asks you to select an app to open the incoming file, as shown in Figure 3.3 (the file being transferred in this case is a PDF document), tap the app you want to use.** Alternatively, you can tap Save to iCloud Drive to save the file to the cloud instead of opening it. Your iPhone completes the transfer and displays or saves the file.

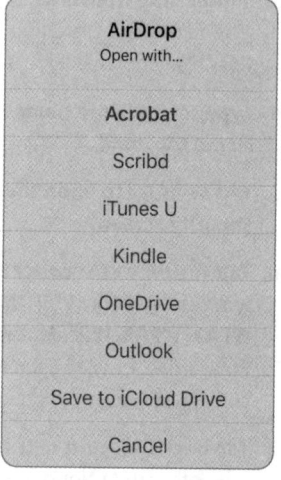

3.3 For some AirDrop transfers, your iPhone asks you to choose an app to open the file.

Forgetting a Wi-Fi network

Having the iPhone remember networks you've joined is certainly convenient, except, of course, when it's not. For example, if you have a couple of networks nearby that you can join, you might connect to one and then realize that the other is better in some way (for example, it's faster or cheaper). Unfortunately, there's a good chance your iPhone will continue to connect to the network you don't want every time it comes within range, which can be a real hassle. Rather than threatening to throw your iPhone in the nearest trash can, you can tell it to forget the network you don't want to use. Here's how it's done:

1. **On the Home screen, tap Settings.** The Settings app appears.

2. **Tap Wi-Fi.** The iPhone opens the Wi-Fi Networks screen.

3. **Tap the blue More Info icon to the right of the network you want to forget.** Your iPhone displays the network's settings screen.

4. **Tap Forget this Network.** Your iPhone asks you to confirm.

5. **Tap Forget.** Your iPhone discards the login data for the network and no longer connects to the network automatically.

Turning off the Wi-Fi antenna

The Wi-Fi antenna on your iPhone is constantly on the lookout for nearby Wi-Fi networks. That's useful because it means you always have an up-to-date list of networks to check out and it makes the iPhone location services (such as the Maps app) more accurate, but it also takes its toll on the iPhone battery. If you know you won't be using Wi-Fi for a while, you can save some battery juice for more important pursuits by turning off the Wi-Fi antenna. Here's how:

1. **On the Home screen, tap Settings.** The Settings app appears.

2. **Tap Wi-Fi.** The Wi-Fi Networks screen appears.

3. **Tap the Wi-Fi switch to Off.** Your iPhone disconnects from your current network and hides the Choose a Network list.

When you're ready to resume your Wi-Fi duties, return to the Wi-Fi Networks screen and tap the Wi-Fi switch to On.

You can also toggle the Wi-Fi antenna off and on by opening the Control Center and then tapping the Wi-Fi icon.

Genius

Setting Up Your iPhone as an Internet Hub

Here's a scenario you've probably tripped over a time or two when roaming around with both your iPhone and your notebook computer. You end up at a location where you have access to just a cellular network, with no Wi-Fi in sight. This means that your iPhone can access the Internet (using the cellular network), but your notebook can't. That's a real pain if you want to do some work involving Internet access on the computer. To work around this problem, you can use a nifty feature called Personal Hotspot, which enables you to configure your iPhone as a kind of Internet hub or gateway device — something like the hotspots that are available in coffee shops and other public areas. To do this, you connect your iPhone to your notebook (either directly via a USB cable or wirelessly via Wi-Fi or Bluetooth), and your notebook can then use the cellular Internet connection of your iPhone to get online. This is often called *Internet tethering*. Even better, you can connect up to five devices to your iPhone, so you can also share your iPhone Internet connection with desktop computers, tablets, other smartphones, and pretty much anything else that can connect to the Internet.

This sounds too good to be true, but it's real, I swear. The downside (you just knew there had to be a downside) is that some providers will charge you extra for tethering. This is slowly changing (for example, AT&T in the United States offers tethering on many of its smartphone plans), but you should read the fine print on your contract to be sure.

Activating the Personal Hotspot

Your first step down the Personal Hotspot road is to activate the feature. Here's how it's done:

1. **On the Home screen, tap Settings.** The Settings app appears.

2. **Tap Personal Hotspot.** iOS displays the Personal Hotspot settings.

3. **Tap the Allow Others to Join switch to On, as shown in Figure 3.4.**

4. **Tap Wi-Fi Password, type a password, and then tap Done.**

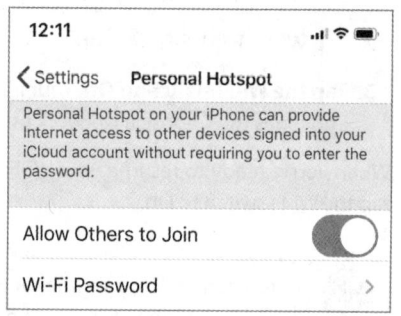

3.4 When the Allow Others to Join switch is On, other people or devices can connect to your iPhone's personal hotspot.

Connecting to the hotspot using Wi-Fi

With Personal Hotspot enabled, follow these steps to allow a device such as a Mac, a PC, or an iPad to use your iPhone Internet connection via Wi-Fi:

1. **On the device, display the list of nearby wireless networks.**

2. **In the network list, click the one that has the same name as your iPhone.** Your device prompts you for the Wi-Fi password.

3. **Type the Personal Hotspot Wi-Fi password and then click OK.** Your iPhone indicates one or more hotspot connections by showing the time with a blue background, as shown in Figure 3.5.

Genius

While the time is highlighted with the blue background, you can tap the time to go directly to the Personal Hotspot settings.

The time is highlighted when you have active hotspot connections

3.5 When you successfully set up a connection to the Personal Hotspot, the iPhone displays a banner showing you how many current connections you have.

Keeping an Eye on Your Data Usage

If you're using your iPhone with a plan that comes with a maximum amount of monthly data and you exceed that monthly cap, you'll almost certainly either pay big bucks for the privilege or have to deal with a slower connection speed. To avoid that, most cellular providers are kind enough to send you a message when you approach your cap. However, if you don't trust that process or if you're just paranoid about these things (justly, in my view), then you can keep an eye on your data usage yourself. Your iPhone keeps track of the cellular network data it has sent or received, as well as the roaming data it has sent or received if you've used your iPhone out of your coverage area.

First, take a look at your most recent bill from your cellular provider and, in particular, look for the dates the bill covers. For example, the bill might run from the 24th of one month to the 23rd of the next month. This is important because it tells you when you need to reset the usage data on your iPhone.

Now follow these steps to check your cellular data usage:

1. **On the Home screen, tap Settings.** The Settings app appears.

2. **Tap Cellular to open the Cellular screen.**

3. **In the Cellular Data section, read the Current Period and Current Period Roaming values.**

4. **If you're at the end of your data period, tap Reset Statistics at the bottom of the screen to start with fresh values for the new period.**

Controlling Network Data

Your iPhone gives you fairly precise control over your network data. For example, you can toggle just the LTE data, all cellular data, data for individual apps, data roaming, or all your iPhone antennas. The next few sections provide the details.

Turning off LTE

Using the LTE cellular network is a real pleasure because it's so much faster than a 3G connection (which in turn is much faster than a molasses-in-January EDGE connection). If LTE has a downside, it's that it uses up a lot of battery power. That's true even if you're currently connected to a Wi-Fi network, because the LTE antenna is constantly looking for an LTE signal. If you'll be on your Wi-Fi network for a while or if your battery is running low and you don't need an LTE cellular connection, you should turn off the LTE antenna to reduce the load on your iPhone battery. Here's how:

1. **On the Home screen, tap Settings.** The Settings app appears.

2. **Tap Cellular.** The Cellular screen opens.

3. **Tap Cellular Data Options.**

4. **Tap Voice & Data.** The Voice & Data screen opens.

5. **Tap 3G.** Your iPhone turns off the LTE antenna in favor of the lower-power 3G antenna.

Turning off cellular data

If you've reached the limit of your cellular data plan, you almost certainly want to avoid going over the cap because the charges are usually prohibitively expensive. As long as you have a Wi-Fi network in range or you're disciplined enough not to surf the web or cruise YouTube when there's no Wi-Fi in sight, you'll be okay. Still, accidents can happen. For example, you might accidentally tap a link in an email message or text message, or someone in your household might use your phone without knowing about your restrictions.

To prevent these sorts of accidents (or if you simply don't trust yourself when it comes to YouTube), you can turn off cellular data altogether, which means your iPhone accesses Internet data only if it has a Wi-Fi signal. Follow these steps to turn off cellular data on your iPhone:

1. **On the Home screen, tap Settings.** The Settings app appears.

2. **Tap Cellular.** The Cellular screen opens.

3. **Tap the Cellular Data switch to Off.**